THE TONGUE HAS ITS
SECRETS

Donna Snyder

NeoPoiesisPress.com

NeoPoiesis Press, LLC

2775 Harbor Ave SW, Suite D, Seattle, WA 98126-2138
Inquiries: Info@NeoPoiesisPress.com
NeoPoiesisPress.com

The Tongue Has Its Secrets
ISBN 978-0-9903565-5-4 (pbk)
    1. Poetry. I. Snyder, Donna.

LOC Number 2016903412

First Edition

Cover Design: Milo Duffin and Stephen Roxborough

Printed in the United States of America.

With many thanks to the writer Ysella Ayn Fulton for over twenty years of encouragement, advice, and friendship

Contents

Part 3

The tongue has its secrets

Praise Her in five songs
a vision of the future written on your tongue
When you look into the mirror to read it
you lean in close   learn it is written backward

The spurt of the mother
a creamy desecration of the dark
The milky way leads through chaos
I follow you   a mirror held in my hand
Behind me   you lead
In front of me   only my own face

Devils at the door
Debris twists in the wind
Darkness begins to subside
Morning sun   reflected in a broken mirror
The words   vaporous signs

Out of devastation new growth green as a jungle
A verdant blanket
Old ones hidden in the dirt
A low voice ringing
The darkness   a promise from the night

Part 1

Masa on the tongue

I want to feed on Corn Maiden's flesh
caramelized in the embrace of mother earth
let it melt on the tongue like agave nectar
rain in the mouth of years to come

Chilling effect[1]

I want to write about being at risk,
silenced and scrutinized.
In nightmares jeweled words
wrangle sense and image.
Sun-shot thought champions dissent,
but anything I say can and will
be used against me.

Why am I alone in this protest?
Where is the vigor of astringency, the vinegar
homilies to warn of Cassandra's oblivion?
Where are the bereaved, clad in weeds
of aubergine & black?
In the garden there is a skein of broken limbs,
bound for burial.
Avert your eyes and pray for solace,
the sweet bitterness of grapefruit marmalade
that wrenches a tongue from slumber.

[1] A chilling effect is the stifling or suppression of political debate or other form of
expression or conduct by creating, through law or force, a fear of penalty or other potential
negative effect. *See, e.g.,* "Chilling Effect Doctrine." *West's Encyclopedia of American
Law* 2005 *Encyclopedia.com.* 15 Apr. 2015

The thieving wind

I can't think now, can't make sense now, can't quit howling and scaring the dogs. Someone sends me a poem lovely with hortensia, blue bloom-filled corners I can't see because wind fills my eyes with grit. My ears and mouth are full of desert. I tell myself that is why I can't hear the voice of the beloved. But there is no beloved, only two unmatched half creatures, or maybe the one is whole in his not-thereness while I am nothing but flaking crepe redolent of fire. The odor of charred flesh and ash chokes me, fills my nose and lungs with something toxic, steals my breath. I hear groans, realize they emanate from my own chest. My flesh desiccates into the scales of a lizard, its tail left inert behind the prickly pear.

Through the pitiless wind a banshee shrieks, Did you not hear me, old woman? No one longs for you, fretting when you are not around. No one reaches for you as solace from the endless gawping nothing that fills the night. No one there but the thieving wind which leaves nothing but the stain of being no one's necessary. No one seeks you, languishing for your touch. Nothing waits but the grave, obscured by shadows beneath a dun sky, heedless of the cry for the comforting hand.

Blue norther'

In the North Texas Panhandle, southbound truckers
blast down Hwy 83, headed to where the wind's not
from the north and not called blue.
Winds and storm outside become Valkyries,
the concrete septic tank a magic stone. Women
warriors ride like furies across the frozen plain.
An Irish woman outruns a chariot,
gives birth to twins,
lays a curse.

The wind takes my spirit in its arms and flees.
Mama lights the candle, locks the door.

Rabbit in the moon

Rabbit looks down,
sees barren land, water infrequent.
The sun's biting caress a death blow.
A cold too vicious to survive without cariño.

Ixchel sent me a lover
but chastity had already claimed me,
denied tactile pleasure and serendipity,
tongue pierced with a cactus spine.

Mariposa sent me a lover,
but I wasn't free to flit from ocotillo
to nopal on wings of pumpkin sun and indigo,
trapped in a box of death the color of plums and sky.

Colibri sent me a lover
who couldn't shimmer in the air drinking sweet.
He plummeted from the sky like a fallen god,
his lungs became rock and his muscles stone.

Jaguar sent me a lover, too,
one kept from me by knives and chains.
He ran into the mountains and lives there still.
You can hear him scream in the starless night.

Eagle sent me a lover
with a tattooed arm that ends in fury,
dead lovers dancing to an unheard drum,
sugar skulls meant to celebrate life reek of death instead.

Rabbit looks down
into this indigo desert, sees my heart twitching
on a plate of lapis and jade, sees blood on the land,
but no succor. No solace. No water to wet my dying tongue.

In search of the one who is waiting

fallen leaves soft as velvet
faded grays and dusky pink
veins dark within decay
humus devoid of warmth
dry leaf upon dry leaf
crushed to powder

infant clouds spun of yucca bloom
a basket woven from Earth's bounty
a future full of mystery and chance
the slow kiss of an aging sun
empty vastness of waiting paper
you give birth to the world
the world becomes your lover

a band of gypsies dancing
the beat of hammers mining
percussive shovels dig into earth
possibly saving your own life

thought deviates from first thought
returns to earth entwined in vine
you want to cry
you see Isis unveiled

Minnow slip of finger

when the artist fell in love
remembering became easier
the way her face looked before he had ever seen it
minnow slip of his finger across her speckled wrist
cinnamon flakes on cream skin
the flush of flesh
humidity sudden in the desert heat
monsoon season of the wet country
here in this country of drought
where death is nearer than life

the old woman appearing like a large baby
draped in blankets color of eggs and wet sand
soles of her feet neglected into rust
look at the desiccating bush
nopales broad and flat and fat
limp crepe easily thought dead
flaccid in the hands of a brutal sun
crushed in its grip

but there amidst all that death
a beard of thorns waits to be trimmed
the ruby flash of tuna
anticipation of eager teeth
dripping sweet

My heart makes chorus with the coyotes

1.
In the cave of leaves I sit counting my toes, each finger
of each hand splaying across my thighs' flesh.
I breathe humid air, cool and green.

2.
It was winter before - difficult, gray, and harsh.
Now new leaves flutter in a sweet breeze.
I rise easily to my feet, graceful as an acrobat.
Strong from yoga, my arms above my head,
my hands describe a technicolor arc.
Breath moves through me.
I am Whitman's song.

3.
A pack of coyotes trill because it's night and the moon
is growing, forgetting that soon they will be a flock
of blackbirds. Birdsong becomes a circle of voices
singing me to death, then back to life.

Out of meaninglessness, words form themselves, blue
leaves entwined about their meaning, an illuminated
manuscript.

Light plays on the rug of shadow spread across the earth.
Blue becomes green, then gray. The moon will wax,
only to embrace its own inevitable loss.

4.
The path to Kin ya 'ah is littered with rain-found shards,
pottery made and used, then trashed, by Anasazi.
The old ones, the Navajo call them. Long thought
a peaceful people, builders and traders, now
some conjecture they engaged in ritual eating
of young flesh.

What is unambiguous is that this tower kiva
rises from a hill and stretches for the moon,
fat above the mesa.

There is silence within the broken medicine
hanging about my neck. Above my head
a bird hunts for supper. I can hear
its wings stroke the somber sky.

Back toward Crownpoint, a Navajo granny herds sheep.
The bell carries to my ear from half mile away,
and I know that it is time to leave this haven.

5.
Winds swirl to bring harmony to sorrow and heal
the sick. My heart makes chorus with the coyotes.
The moon above the mesa prepares to disappear.

Dea tacita

Lara's tongue severed by the sky for indiscretion
Love led her on a spiral path deep into the laurel
She gave birth to little gods but was forever silent

She lingers at cross roads
Tends the dead

Tiny truths hidden

keep the hand moving fast
distract the eye
como el mago or an alchemist
a practitioner of legerdemaine
can it be trickery and not be a lie?

tiny truths hidden like contraband
troublemakers named on a secret list
the names of all your connects
criminals
subversives
deviants of every stripe
even the grandmothers who walk in the plaza
grieving their young who disappeared by force
how many dead in the back of a truck?
how many dumped in the reeking maw
of some city with subtitles?

if I told you I would have to kill you
then where would I be?
naked in the brush
a thorned and predatory habitat
here even lifeless gardens hold broken glass
with dead fingers

I am wandering in a wilderness
the refuge others speak of eludes me
I sniff the dizzying secrets of the sibyl
No news is good news
she hisses in my ear
malodorous air swirls around me
my eye distracted by a flash of red

Seven deer seven times

I walked in the Sandia foothills
chilled by the first wintry wind,
half moon in a dusky sky, arroyo
luminous with profligate datura.
Rocky watermelon brilliance
dizzied me with sheer geometric bulk.

Snakes slept beneath the earth. Plumed
grass danced a winter rite. Seven deer
crossed my path seven times.

I lay on a rock before the mother stone,
sole offering the salt and breath of my flesh.
My back to the world in the valley below me,
I stopped time.

Prestidigitation

Distract the masses from the moving hand Torture women in front of Mylar to bad Motown music Doves fly from the silken hat Colored scarves flutter, to entertain the eye Hands beneath the table and behind the screen

See the doves fly through the air, grace in every feather Held aloft by something like magic Minute muscles Quills filled with air

Air within Air below Air above Presto Magico the magician has won

The adept infuses artifice with sufficient awe skeptics suspend disbelief We are not so much fooled as enchanted in the way old Irish adepts cast glamours A body disappeared, reappeared at will Shapes shifted before the very eye Before bells had ceased to chime a tale was born

This is how the world began Creatures flying against a wintry sky A single feather drifting downward

Outstretched fingers Voices calling The echo of bells recede into the wind Dogs whimper struggling to decode the senses A bird's wings whisper

Eternal return

So she took a lover. (Or did the lover take her? Isn't truth overrated anyway?) So many years passed between then and now, the painting in the attic old and oozing, the two of them strangers. She's grown a beard in solidarity with a dying dog, wind sand-blasted straight to the eye of god. No more moisture, neither kind welcome.

Death's infinite return, the universe sucked into its own black hole. Nothingness and nowhere somewhere on the other side of somethingness. Give thanks for gravity, despite the bags and sags, the drooping down. Gravity, in the end, is our salvation. There on the lip of nowhere, Gravity dons unitard and cape and saves the day. That is, saves the universe. Some version of something returns as we bounce higher, farther than the reach of energy and matter. Begin again. There was an old man named Michael Finnegan, dead long ago, but the wake continues.

Carnality will resume after this break for station identification. Only the shadow knows for sure. The dying daddy wanted to know, what is love, anyway? She wonders as she wanders through time and space if he ever knew before his last breath, or at any time when young. She wonders when will the widows ever learn, pity is not compassion. A helping hand is not commitment. Lust will die.

The first question answered, there is nothing more to say.

Feathers floating in the grease

Even my angels flee these tears inescapable as my shadow. A shaky lot, they've fallen to the inhospitable embrace of dust, wrestled to Earth by Jacob. They weep blood, wings become scarlet scab, flowers clenched between teeth.

Did you hear about the one who tattled? She whispered in my ear things I should know but never wanted to hear, betrayed for less than a mess of lentils. Cold beans.

I might never have known the truth except somebody handed me the key to Blackbeard's closet of deceit. I hated it enough when I was just a dirty little secret. Now I am supine before the ignominious truth. My name is only one among a horde of others, all on queue to kiss and scream and never tell. This time no strength in numbers.

The others disappear into a book of shadowed faces. I am left alone with the shame of being unable to suppress my sorrow, lying in a puddle of slime, an empty bowl of lentil soup still in the kitchen sink, feathers floating in the grease.

Your words a string of drunken pearls

1.

You came with murmurs, soft and slurred, compelling me to know those arms, inhale the scent of your sweaty back, tactile remnants of unspoken lies. But you never told me what was at stake, merely some stifled talk of you and me, impossible to know just what you meant. You chanted my name in rhythms unforetold before you came and raised the stakes, your words a string of drunken pearls at my throat.

The Misfits' lyrics in the background underscored your message, a moment like this never lasts, a hybrid moment part fantasy finally realized, part waking dream, and understandings based on tacit promises seldom hold. Yet only you were strong enough to force the moment, to dare disturb the fragmented universe we had known. Your whisky lips burned a path for me to follow, your callused hands a torch to show the way. I hid my scars behind fingers tired of death, tears marring the doleful satin of my shirt.

2.

You call me mi'jita. You call me mi niña. Across my shoulders, small fires bloom wild. Your legs are twin pillars holding up the sky. Your eyes, twin furies, demand I meet your gaze, no time to create a face to hide behind.

You refuse to avert your eyes from my dying body wrapped in its soiled sheet. I shut my eyes but you still see me. Your arms a home in which I am a guest only. You sit me on a pillow, fetch me buttered toast and tea. I find a pair of loaded dice in the bottom of the cup.

Blue sky way

A brown bird flies me
beyond the turquoise sky
In that distant land a red stone
shows me the way to a new home
where I have lived since creation
It shows me the blue sky way
where mountains know me
even before I speak my name

I am the medicine you need
a gift from a woman crazed by knowing
The man with bloodied hands behind me

Dried plants in an old basket
gather power while you sleep
There is picture of an archangel
A demon's mask with blue eyes
You may turn your back on me
You may deny that I am in you
but truth is found in the way
I fly through the air
Land upright on a Navajo rug
Magic around my belly
Spells across my back

Hear me rumble truth in your deepest sleep

My tears are spines on cactus

desert nights consume all moisture
leave nothing but crepe paper for skin
no pen to write across my back
no paint to disguise my fleshy shame
sad clown mouth that's below the belt
I tell myself big girls don't cry but I lie
I just cannot go gentle
although I suffer my share of rage

my muse wears a fuck-off bracelet
black leather with silver studs
she knows how to use it to good effect
her rejections affect my mood
me repudiated and left with nothing
just this endless bitter day-after pill
each airless morning worse than the next
my fingers scream with her not thereness
me wrapped in a soiled sheet
like Lazarus before Jesus came to the party
You can smell me
acrid
deadness fills my vacuoles

I hear her summon me in my sleep
when I wake up she slaps me
calls me silly
she oils her leather boots and strap-on
I lie in bed
without

my tears are spines on cactus
wishing for a good rain

A little bit Rapunzel

I am my family's restitution
given over to Herself as comfort
Herself the ugly aspect of the Mother
fierce jailor jealous and obscene

voice and charm my only blessings
I braid escape from enforced solitude
birds teach me the way in their own language

Make a prayer in rhyme and meter

smell the acrid winds blowing through flame
feel the sway of the hanged man
listen to words and know their unfortunate meaning
know the bloody root
make a prayer in rhyme and meter
bury it beneath a gate named Shelagh
look into the light on the lip of the wave
salute the bastard wounds of a dying moon

Part 2

Prepare to ululate

Stare the beast in the face, there in the mirror.
Notice the ten-armed monster,
the sleek skin of its fleshy tentacles
wrapped tight around your throat chakra,
not quite asleep where it has overrun
your heart chakra,
pulsating in the center of your root chakra,
its skin red-black in the refracted light.

Force the air through your throat.
Awaken your voice.
Laugh out loud.
Spell out the meaning--let
mirth grow into a cackle.
Cast the spell.
Use ALL CAPS for emphasis.

The subtle grace of the crone
at the core of the principle of beauty.
The end cycles into a beginning.
Tentacles ripple into wakefulness.
Feel your throat dilate.
Prepare to ululate.
Feel the giant squid moving in the secret dark.

Let your voice burst through the deep
like exploding stars.

The peacock's scream

I wanna return to a home never mine
Peacocks in a deep green garden
Sweet smells slithering over skin

Mama stands here
Twisted vines link her belly to mine
Her red lips a pin-up's smile
Skin sparkling like antifreeze on concrete
Iridescent waves of heat off the sidewalk

The land here stretches all the way to Oklahoma
Red dirt baked under a sorry ass sun
First one vine
then another
sprout from the cracked earth
Dark green

Mama disappears into the waiting earth,
red and angry

Mama disappears into the waiting earth

Mama disappears and I am left behind
heat broken only by a peacock's scream

Struggling with fragile

bones of the broken moon turn verdant
flesh and sinew become roaming beasts
spilled blood becomes life
she is the moon who decorates her face
with rattlesnakes

broken into strange shapes
she quivers
calls forth the waters to flood and surge
makes the blood rush forth between the legs

the fragile moon
her body broken
her bones and body become life

Dreaming in mother of pearl

small breasts and rolls of fat
body of immortal pulchritude
Goddess of love and righteous indignation
she rose fleshy and pristine from the foam
of the infinite sea

unlike Athena
born from the imperfect brow of the father
Aphrodite is perfect
unmeasured and without flaw

her image transcends the span of time
small breasts and fat rolls
blood and breath surge through my mortal body
I close my eyes and dream in mother of pearl

Invoking the muse

she who can write on a dime
purveyor of instant poetry
written on the spot
words never fail her
she speaks words
and coffee drinkers quit stirring their cups
illicit lovers break gaze
waitresses grab pens and scribble on scraps
words zing like neon tracers through the air
poetry happens

boys turn shy and think of woman
she who speaks words of power
an aspect of the triple goddess
she who embodies abundance

maker of kings
caster of spells
inciter of riots

she who wields the power of words

Beauty uncaptured

1.

a golden frame empty
an aqua wall embellished with a subtle vignette
creamy rich mat frames nothing
a piece of aqua enclosed within a line of gold
the image supplied
as in all instances of beauty beheld
projected from the eye of the beholder

empty wall the aqueous amniotic fluid
the vignette on golden frame froth of waves
golden in the sunlight

2.

born from the infinitely available and varied sea
sun-gilded waves recede and swell
promise of ceaseless pleasure

beauty uncaptured
neither ransomed nor bought nor yet possessed
free of the ownership of gods or fathers
since Time severed Heaven's cock

behind the golden frame only aqua wall

3.

a plate of pits the morning after
grape skin peeled by teeth
suckled by tongue and lips
sweetness rolling down
throat and chin

the moment remembered
the swallowed moment
the moment spent

Fat beauty

There next to the mirror encrusted with shells
is propped the photograph of la Roseanne.
Annie Liebowitz shot a series of Rosanne,
abundant flesh beautiful in its vastness,
black lace bleeding across her corpulence.
She lolls across a bed like a painting by Botero.
Lush fruit in its glossy glory demands the caress
of moist lips. When you look at her genuine beauty,
Roseanne's fat beauty of abundance, appetite
swirls through you like steam in a sauna,
eddies near your chubby ankles moist and hot.
The mirror might sing your praise, but for the memory
of dieting eight year olds who would rather be maimed
or stupid than be fat. For them, the mirror weeps.

You light a candle before Roseanne's picture. Notice
la Guadalupe looks chunky too, in her pink gown
and starry cloak. You light a candle to Liebovitz,
who recognizes beauty comes in all sizes
and makes her art reflect that truth.
You look in the mirror with its trim of shells,
and laugh with the memory of just the other day,
striding through the market so full of strength
all the vendors turned to stare. Boys slipped
you grins like magic potions, charms for your altar,
offerings to the image of la Roseanne.

Three sides of the same moon

When there is no moisture, no frigid
desert air or vapors off a hot river,
night easily deceives the eye. Dark
drenches mesas with brilliance, midnight
snowscapes under the summer moon.
While she waxes you perceive depth in shadow,
dark passages to nowhere but where you are.

In the third cycle, love tricks sight.
The over-ripeness of bruises,
blemishes. All the defects veiled,
diffused in twilight

Rainbow girl

brown bugs crawl across Rainbow Girl's face
she holds the sacred plant and faces east
leads the people on the rainbow way
hagoneh
thank you
it is good

time is that way
leaves you behind in a velvet blouse
looking at silver hairs in the mirror
the young ones call you shimasani
grandmother
ancient one
one who talks for all
the powerful one
mother of the world

Coyote grins
he knows moonlight will come again
spread its milky fingers over rock and mesa
Rainbow Girl bows into the wind
earrings dangle turquoise teardrops for her people

the future is a blue glass bottle
break it if you will
or use it to catch tears to drink
when rain forget it loves sky
and brown bugs no longer crawl
across paintings in the sand

Faith wants to dance

her eyes tell me she will never forget
she repeats "we must do something!"
tells me of her twenty-five year marriage
her husband once a free thinking hippie
now a sober and moody elected official
each night she tells me he watches TV
after a full day working she has to cook

puny frame
thirsty flesh
skin painfully aware he does not want her
Faith wants to dance
she wants to be eaten with a spoon
her flesh quaking
his voice a whisper

she trembles with the memory of his desire
she's not too old to recall humidity in a dry world
caresses like little birds flying across her skin
her eyes are gray clouds in a pale sky
one thing she tells me she will never forget
that night he told her she was not his first choice
she wishes he hadn't settled for second best
she wishes he would leave her alone when she is lonely
she wishes he would just touch her with affection
she never meant to get old
she never wanted to become not worth the effort

I wish she could touch herself gently until she screams
relentless erotic melancholy of tango on the stereo
champagne on the bathroom counter
cotton panties hanging on the corner of the bed

Vernal

Now is the time of miracles
Eos wings through persimmon dawn
Astarte strokes her favorite hare
Freya dressed in gossamer and wreath
Saraswati holds her lotus bloom
Isis restores her lover to life
The blood of Cybele's lover
gives us violets before his resurrection
Soon the Passion of the Son of Mary
She of the Sacred Heart

Crones stretch gnarled fingers
no longer cramped by bitterness
It is the time to clean and sow
Long light and short night return
Seeds planted in cold dark give birth

Bitter poison of history denied

the sound of wind through leaves has changed
birds don't know where to nest
now the young trees are dying

a small house made of poisoned timbers
a mother gathers vipers
puts them in a basket woven of stunted limbs

for her anger to be owned
she would need to see the malice
there in the mirror that hangs beside her bed

eyes averted from books from an unknown pen
she chooses not to hear the message grackles bring
instead castigates the birds for being noisy and black

she turns her back on history written by a dark hand
relegates to myth the wisdom of the tide
daylight filters through trees losing their life blood

waves move the moon to madness
quiet the vipers' hissing anger
the bitter poison of treeless night

Earth Day

If I were the Earth,
I would lose myself
to intermittent plagues of despair.
How could I not?
I travel among my People,
in the land of canyons, mesas, and buttes.
Here I weep and rage (have you heard?)
to see the ravages of wars of attrition
waged in the name of energy and profitability.
I travel among my People
in the land of this once grand river valley,
fragile desert, and these dying mountains.
Here I weep and rage (have you not seen?)
for toxins replace nutrients necessary to harbor life.

I am exhausted by the ravages of war
waged in the name of progress.
Poisonous disregard and knowing acts
foul the flow of my big river.
Babies are born with kidneys outside the body
rather than their natural place, born without brains
because mamas drank brave waters,
corrupted by evil both seen and unseen–
pesticides, radioactive isotopes, carcinogens.

If I were the Earth,
I would sometimes succumb
to violent rages against perversity,
perpetrators' flippant disregard for senseless horror.
Perhaps I could become inured
to tragedy and comedy,
oblivious to horror and terror.
But then I would regret
that greater harm befalls me
than the villain of this story.
As long as I can be cataclysmically annoyed,
maybe I can regain my strength.

If I were the Earth,
I would long for sleep--the kind where a breeze
caresses me with clean air and shows me
how I am blessed.
With such sleep, I could persist,
continue to have random flashes
of lucid dreams and surreal clarity,
fortuitous gushes of brine,
floods of clear water.

If I were the Earth,
I would fling off gravity's leash,
careen wildly through the universe
until I found a safe place
where I could sleep and play,
rain sweet water
into my own waiting body,
whirl again among my sisters in the sky.

The Sunday news

1.

From the Associated Press
Dolphins found shot, slashed, stabbed.
Mutilations recorded in recent months.
One had a hole made by a 9 mm bullet.
Marine scientists report four stranded.
Another found dead on Deer Island,
a piece of his jaw missing.

This just in
Nietzsche was right about God. I am alone
in an incomprehensible world. Sentient
creatures that might have the answer I seek die
bleeding peace into a dirtied ocean, waters fouled
with despair that cannot be scrubbed clean.

Dateline Damascus
Children and journalists mutilated and killed by bombs,
blown into the meaningless abyss of a zero sum game.
They failed to learn the rules of play.

In other news
People shot, slashed, stabbed--
an endless litany of horror born of greed.

Next up, commentary
Nothingness lurks behind image and word.

2.

Tears of God fall brittle upon the fat of my cheek
as from a frozen deity, stripped of omniscience,
denuded of omnipotence, omnipresent no more.
An arrowless quiver, body unflung at its mark,
I wait for the somethingness, something born
of the limbs of the mother of all gods. She
whose breast will protect me. She who will take me
into brown arms and cover me with a blanket of green
in a nearly endless blue, spinning through infinite dark.

In the land of birdsong

Past
The influence of the siren song long past.
Women dressed in yellow petals,
bosoms like islands,
bare feet planted firmly in red sky.

The air smells of green fronds and sweat.
Women call out like ringing bells,
the secret places wide open.
Sailors are weak from hunger,
wishing for beds hidden in trees.

Present
A peacock goddess subsumes my present,
stroking my face with magenta and indigo.
The deep red sex of woman screams with hunger.

A royal bird gives me the plumes of her mate,
wrapping me in a robe of eyes so that I may see
my here, my now, my forest for the trees.

Future
In the land of birdsong I intone the colors of the world.
Fire on my head does not consume the jelly brain.
Some wear masks and hint of warfare.
Our future listens to the language of birds,
hand held out in peace while battles lurk.
We are all comandantes here.

Dress me in every color. I will make war
in the name of freedom.

Blood turns to ocean, bones to trees.

Carmine

Intimate touch. Communication spirit to spirit by way of flesh. This is my body. Take it and weep. This is your blood. Baptize me in its sorrow. Most likely this story will end like all the rest, death stacked upon death, either that of the beloved or our own.

We stand each day before the catafalque. Only the willful or ignorant are blind to our inexorable demise, each gnarl of the tree trunk a divergent path to that certain end. Evanescence hovers, feathers dropping, carmine skin raw as chewed flesh. Breath and thought incarnate. Eyes weep drops of blood before a tapestry of souls we failed to save.

Trace the plump curve of a youthful cheek, the delicate swirl of ear. Follow each breath, chests moving in unison. Then one by one we leave ourselves behind, shredded by the desert wind.

Bear who loves a woman

1.
Bear lies down and dreams, smells Female on the way.
maybe she comes from the other side of the Moon.
maybe she makes her way to this side of All That Is.
he hears his blood moving through his ears,
tastes her menses, feels it painted on his cheeks.
at midnight the stars themselves show him her face,
and then he wakes.

2.
around her neck hangs a bear.
when she wears the color blue, black ribbon
holds it in the sky, between her breasts.
she wears it on a field of black when she needs
its strength.

she moves through a forest, without family or home.
when she awakens to her hunger, it is cold and dark.
she moves slowly through ill-lit thoroughfares, thirsts,
has an itch to scratch. around her neck hangs a fetish,
brown and imperfect.

3.
Bear moves across the Earth,
his sole aim to meet the needs of his body.
he moves through the night, finds her asleep
in the dark place of his own mind.

4.
she responds to the throaty urgency in his voice.
her flesh moves toward his without intent. he
fits her body to his, turns her over in his arms,
breathes into her ear. she wakes cradled
in the arms of the night sky.

5.
Bear mouths her flesh,
mutters little truths into her neck and back.
calls her flesh Mama, calls her his Daughter.
her story cannot be told,
a mystery unrevealed,
a knowledge unknowable.

Serpent wraps itself in Moon's crown

Ixchel wears Serpent on her head
wrapped into her crown.
She outlines the paintings on its back,
glyphs made from an ancient root,
serpentine remnants of a stellar past.
Serpent's caress falls like a feather on air,
its tongue flicking ravaged skin in reminder
of allure long succumbed
to the predations of jungle.

No thorned or stinging barrier can bar Serpent's touch,
snaking beneath, below, and over, raising its head
from the darkness, touching softly the secret places,
unafraid of the moon.

The dancer

the woman is a fetish
all bellies and breasts
air caresses her hips
she moves across the floor
like undulating silk
like the Ayasofya mosque
if it were to sway through Istanbul

the scents of the Egyptian market cling
to arabesques of air that flow around her
her strength and grace move me
pleasure finds me
freed of the burden of corporeality
I dance

Part 3

On listening to Gertrude Stein, the smell of fresh rosemary on my tongue

I am hiding in his mama's garden,
sitting in the middle of a patch of herbs,
dill and garlic gone wild like dancers
eager to fill every spot of the ballroom floor.

I threw on a soiled dress, ran outside to hug the earth,
lest it fling itself out of the orbit of the sun
and leave me crying, in a garden where none know me.
Naked behind the cloth, thin denim
separates my flesh from blackest soil.
My bare feet are happy white orchids
kissed with a trace of blue.

It is here I know best that I must die.
"If I told him, would he like it?
Would he like it if I told him?"
I linger in her garden, hungry
for the bitter taste of herb against my eager tongue.

The earth is my only solace, black and ancient.
But once and once and once again,
in the story of his heart I lived out loud,
I lived big.
"If I told him, would he like it?
Would he like it if I told him?"

Out loud?
Out loud and big?

Lingua ignota

for Hildegard of Bingen

the less common than *a*
lingua ignota with its litterae ignotae
Hildegard's Latinate Rheinlandish code
its DNA of phantasms and hierarchy of flowers
a secret discourse of herbs and angels

a hidden language of sisters
confessors and confidantes
linguistic hierarchy with words of symbol
spies everywhere thus her secret language
Benedictine rules used to bend Vatican law
near saint yet transgressive
emanations of her glory extend
far beyond Rhineland and Rome
beyond continents and centuries

Jutta recognized her uncommon student
who created letters and prayed in music
Hildegard perpetuated quiescence to give voice
hierarchical language hidden from the hierarchs
truth found in rapture
the efficacy of folk remedies
the flourishing of tacit thought
her effulgence covert therefor unsuppressed

nothing in her mind not first in heaven's nature
terrestrial flora more common than celestial vision
a more common than *the*

Monstrous angel

for the Russian painter, Pavel de Nikolaev

Brown-eyed angel.
Smudged wings, lavender gray,
drape from sloped shoulders.
Course-spun tunic trimmed with lyres.
A field of lilac. A determined mouth,
pursed. Red with readiness. Domed
eyes the size of elbows. A gabled brow.
Twice as large as her round head,
a flat earth, trees and houses for a crown.
Upstretched arms hold the earth steady.
Legs splayed, bare feet point
toward the ground below her.
A city at her knees, each window
illuminated in gold.

Both unearthly and of this earth,
she has a secret. She carries the world
on her head. She is the X that marks the spot.

The Nǚ Shu poets

a silken dress obscures the secret skill of a poet
as she walks before portraits in a Taoist temple
envy of male scholarship celebrated empirically
she writes her longing in a secret women's language
wistful for her friend, she croons of summer mountains

a fisherman's child-wife sent her secret lessons
as if she were a boy slated for imperial examination
words threaded through letters or disguised
in basketfuls of cultivated flowers
broken and bound prettily like feet

in thanks, she sends a scarf embroidered with a sea creature
her poem hidden in plain view, woven in silk thread
as if together, delight rings loud as waves in the blood of both

lowered eyes see shoes given by her lord and husband
tonight she will dream of wild tentacles, a hungry mouth
in the morning sea salt will trace her murmuring lips

Escape on the back of Epona's child

her sentence imposed by a fearful mind and harsh hand
a forest of knives and poison plants better than razor wire
men armed with madness patrol the far reach of pleasure
nothing more suspect than a happy woman
inspect her closely with nose and eye
or suspicious ear

the horse runs toward dark water like her own child
his eyes reflect the secrets of a reemerging moon
her thighs grasp his naked haunches
his flesh and muscle become her secret power
a milky way leads to infinity's other side
she heads for the far edge of the high desert
fleeing hunger and castigation
night skies ripple shadows on a still lake

she follows the runes inside her eyelids
her voice a promise of daylight and freedom
ties that bind wait for her return
bonfires doused in the pagan night
rituals ridden into an unforgiving dust

Invoking Oshun

I find myself beside a dying river
the sound of copper bells leads me
From my mouth to yours
I say as I drip her honey
into the Rio Grande
then lick my sweet fingers
the river accepts her honey
it falls from my flesh
and is gone

wind laughs through the cane

Flora has fled

The young ones see the futility of her quest, unavailing as that which led to the influx of Spaniards into the land of Tequesta and Seminole 500 years ago. Ponce de Leon proved himself as big a fool, prowling through the land of flowers looking for a fountain of perpetual youth. Now she seeks a mirror full of fresh blooms, searches the glass for the one she used to see there after she was loved completely. She would lean into the mirror, whispering wondrous agreement with words offered by her lover mere moments earlier.

Flora does not smile within this frame. No one there but herself, pendulous jowls beneath sagging lids, a ruff of fat beneath the chin. Flora has fled. No one home but this stranger in the mirror. This hag, this crone, waiting for wisdom.

The truth of Vikings

The music in her head makes her scared,
as if Vikings still brandished their blades
from the decks of ships fierce as dragons.
Afloat in an ageless river,
the leaves are chill flames.
Cold rains obscure the water's source,
hiding it away like the secret of a woman's
aging body, rain, a woman's sluggish heat.
She is apples and pears ripened
in her own sweet skin.
Only the moon can match
the luster of her opalescent belly.
Her mouth makes shadows. Her hair
a burning bush. Her fingers a doorway,
iconic as a religious artifact. She is on route
to the end of being on the back of a red swan,
on the way to nothingness made tolerable
by ritual and fire.

Through the wind, she hears the shriek
of disconsolate women who no longer
believe love will save them from sorrow.
There is no home now, they wail.
There is no safe place.
Death tastes like winter flowers.
She knows this because she knows
things she is not supposed to know.
She stands so close she can hear
warriors tell each other secrets.
The truth is that neither love nor death
diminishes you. The way to truth
is a life suffered, a drunken waltz.
She stands so close her howl is lost
in the roar of music inside her head.
She is wordless before the fact of Vikings,
truth found in a harsh yellow light.

Aqua de mi sierra madre™

the label shows a mountain
silvered with age
valleys deepened with shadow
subtle green and gray
azured in the twilight
an origin story filtered
through memory of stone
eroded by the rough edge of time
mi sierra madre trademarked
her water held by plastic

there are no ripples
natural to a plastic shell
if you hold it to your ear
nothing whispers to you
if you put it to your lips
no one kisses you
there is no mother there
no flowers draped
across stone mountains
volcanic necks unadorned
no verdant growth of spring
no clean water cooling
my overheated flesh

nothing but a sip of water
stolen from a spring
sold for pieces of plata
a dollar and some change

Lament for Mother Crow

Sold
for 106,000 Euros, $209,000 American,
more than three times the pre-sale estimate
because calamity sells, you know. Headlines
sell. It's the American way, and apparently
the French way, but not the Hopi way.

Stolen
by a Frenchman 100 years ago,
She brings bean sprouts to The People,
peaceful desert-dwellers who live in mud houses
or trailers, there in the bellybutton of the world.
She initiates children into the life before them,
ensures their good health and behavior, blesses them.

An elder
brands the sale a crime against The People,
the Hopi, their pueblo surrounded by Others.
Encircled by a hostile Navajo Nation.
Enclosed by the usurping State of Arizona.
Swallowed by the United States of America.
Vomited out in Paris on an auction block.

Mother Crow
brings life to the Hopi each year. She
is mother of all the kachinas who bring
water from the mountains so blue corn
will grow and be ground into meal,
baked into piki, thin wisps of blue bread
that crumble and melt on the tongue.

Her spirit
in the feathered wooden mask, religious relic
carved and painted, adorned with turquoise stone,
pieces of godliness. The embodiment of Mother Crow,
sold to the highest bidder somewhere cold,
somewhere not the center of the earth,
too far for Her to fly back to Her mountain
and return next year at the appointed time.

Jocasta

Jocasta
Hands dyed carmine
Hennaed lyrics strident in her head
A son's love births widows and fratricide

The trials of women
Conundrums finessed
Loves stolen by man or fate
Their riddles answered by their own death

A man blinded by lust for his mother
He rips himself from the womb of her desire
His seeds fall into the earth like dragon teeth
Drama waters earth's green plain

The flash of his dagger
Fatalism of a female no longer dewy with wonder
At the inopportune moment truth revealed as truth
Drama made comedy with the mere turn of a face

The muse of Juárez

1. Bodies of girls scattered

Somebody killed the muse.
Last seen lying in an alley, tongue
severed, served in tacos on the street.
Eyeballs, naked as glass without paint,
tossed to a boy huddled on the curb.
Lids stitched to eyebrows. Nose
cut off to spite her face, thrown
into the salsa at La Cometa.

Finger tips scorched by poison.
Wrists tied behind her back,
hands bound with a bungee cord.
The softest flesh scored with the tip
of a butcher knife. Her words, ash
in the back seat of a burned-out car.

Girls immobilized. Senses stunned
into senselessness. Panties knotted
around necks. Mamas' grief
gone dry and mute as the desert.

This empty lot on the edge of J-town[1].
Its unmistakable stench of ruined flesh.
Bodies of women scattered like seed
of desert shrubbery, sown in dead stones.

2. An old woman's body

Somebody killed the muse,
replaced her sense of self
with endless shame. Showed
her herself, repulsive.

Dying flesh. Overpowering stench.
Flaccid skin. The gaping hole,
ignominy of an old woman's body.

Again, a severed tongue. Body twisted
into a shape unholy and irreparable.
Consigned to a twilight of inutility and shame.

No offer of caress or shelter. Life stolen
because death was coming anyway, always,
without resurrection.

3. *The sound of blackbirds*

Somebody killed the muse, her words trampled
beneath the feet of savages, beneficent touch stolen,
inexorably replaced with a current of living death,
soon enough to be dying breath.

A figment of irrepressible self now gone.
No more reprieve than mercy.
The hidden well contaminated.
The world silent. A dead stone.

Nothing but the sound of blackbirds cawing,
crying out in grief.

---

[1] J-town is a nickname for Juárez, México, where hundreds of girls and women have been
murdered and mutilated in what has been called femicide.

At La Mayapan

Mayan symbols watch me from the wall and tabletop.
I wait for sopa de berros con bolitas. Whole corn
kernels enrich its broth, cajole the cold inside me
to remember who I was and who I am. Good corn
masa dumplings remind me even redheads can invoke
the Corn Maiden's blessing. Bolitas de masa,
tortilla de maíz, sweet tamal. Transubstantiation
lets Her body nourish me. She comforts me,
reminds me that in this world I am flesh and blood.

My comadre says Mayan prophecy unfolds in our time.
As for me, I can't see beyond my bowl of soup.
Steam caresses my cheek, reminds me of El Gustito,
how its ecstatic Jorocho harp screams with pleasure.
Somewhere in Burque, Daddy mourns his autonomy,
the pleasure of vigor. He wanders in and out of sleep,
never seems to wake. There is a hole inside me corn
cannot fill. I don't know what goes there, who I was,
who I am, who I may become.

I search for solace but remain bereft,
ask for meaning but there's a bad connection.

The Perfecter

1.
A genderless soul
A radiant spirit meditates on how and when

Four paths
Petals of truth mark the way
Spiraling signs of the triple goddess omnipresent

The universe dreams of you
Integration more than perfection

The ultimate outcome
The final destination
Aspiration more than prescriptive

2.
A caldron
A sword
A spear
A stone pillar
The effulgent universe held within

Three candles of illumination

The basis of the issue
A woman astride a boat abundant with spring's bounty
Eyes closed, she sails beneath the waning moon of hope's grief
In the fearful dark a siren sings of green cloth on a man's head
She plays the strings of every hearing heart with her left hand
Chants of a woman who moves horses across a sunset-painted sea
Her strength will enable the necessary outcome

The truth of the matter
A dancing girl hides love beneath a scarlet hat
Eyes down, she gives herself over to her innate nature
If she were not flesh and blood she would hold a dove
It would feel peace in the shelter of this benevolent breast
In the pomegranate's juice hidden knowledge swells
A mother holds a daughter as the poet's oracle foretold

The third candle of illumination
Daughter Spring blooms under a waxing moon
Mother Harvest reveals the full moon's bounty
Half Moon Crone embodies growing shadow
The third candle illuminates the darkness at hand

Creation myth

1.Woman smiles

Woman smiles, her face starred,
exotic birds tattooed around her mouth,
beneath her eyes, around her nose.
Delicate teeth exposed to heaven,
confident no one will scorn.

Woman smiles at Okie brothers, Indian lovers.
Grandmas squat over iron pots of lard and lye.
Good black river bottom, green with growth--
the kind that feeds and chokes,
the kind that covers graves.

Candles flicker. Drums beyond the wall.
Fiddles call jumping boys who prance and chant,
scaring away the spirits.

Rain on a tin roof.
Honeysuckle raising Cain on the side porch.
Dogs under the floor boards, warm and waiting.

Woman smiles--
a wedding vase, a water bird, a box of roots.
A rocking horse. A basket facing east.
Out of the earth a mist floats
and fondles the turtle and the deer.

Stars on her face--Woman smiles.
Beads on her head--Woman smiles.
Bird at her chin--Woman smiles.
Stone in her pocket--Woman smiles.
Rainbows behind her--Woman smiles.

Behind the mask, we find Woman.
And once truly found, Woman smiles.

2. *Creation*

A fairy hands me beads and wee bells on a string.
Fairy bells, he says, winding them about my neck.
They hang down my chest, promise a cool breeze,
and gray clouds to hide the new blue sky.

Bells tinkle and tell of a place where God
smiles and pulls the world from between her legs.
A turtle escapes a thoughtless lunch,
wilted lettuce and white bread in an iron pot.
His home painted on his back, his jaws break twigs.
Scaly feet carry him over the roots of elms and sumac.
He traces his bottom and tail across rich, black earth.

God bends to stroke the back of Turtle, her vast bottom,
turned up to the sky, extends to infinity--quite a spread!
God smiles at the world—blue oceans,
persimmon clouds, continents green and black.
She has dogs named China and India.
China! she calls, *India!* The sweet dogs crowd
around her knees. Make her dance.

3. *Dream*

I dream of God lying on the earth,
beneath a warm sun. A cool breath of wind
strokes the soft skin of her thighs and neck.
A fairy whispers in my ear that God
is a woman at all times being pleasured.
Out of her pleasure unfolds the world.

Willendorf

breasts sag without symmetry
pendulous bellies attest to use
braided face of the mysteries
an erotic fetish carried by the faithful
small enough to fit in the palm
or carry on a thong about the neck
always available to caress and fondle

a prayer for abundance and fecundity
buried beneath a bed of pine bough

always here inside my head

Supplication

O great and beneficent energy flow,
cast out that which is an abomination
to my spirit. Envelope me in your electric
aura. Lend me its protection and strength.
Restore my vitality. Make it pure and sweet.

Heal my wounds with your tears. Give me
technicolor visions at midday and ¡por favor!
a safe haven in the night.
Cloak me with your starry mantle.
Cool my fever with your caress.
Bring to my cheek the scent of rain,
the sweet breath of clover.

In the morning, feed me honey with fresh yogurt,
and mint or sage tea at noon.
In the evening, stroke me
with the peacock feathers
of your benevolence.

Remind me of the sweetness of my existence
in your heart. Keep me from ugliness. Lead
me to recognize splendor in all its guises.

Forget not my friends or my enemies.
Bring peace with valor to my soul.

Blessed be your presence throughout infinity.

Acknowledgements

Earlier versions of some of these poems have appeared in various journals, anthologies, and blogs. I thank the editors of those publications for their generous support.

Boboland Cronicas
Boston Poetry Magazine
Carcinogenic Poetry
El Paso Bar Journal
I Am Not a Silent Poet
Matrix
Mezcla
Montucky Review
Newspaper Tree
Return to Mago
Sin Fronteras
Unlikely Stories 2.0
VEXT Magazine.

About the Author

Donna Snyder's work as an activist lawyer advocating on behalf of indigenous people, immigrant workers, and people with disabilities has garnered multiple prizes and recognitions. In 1995 she founded the grassroots, not-for-profit *Tumblewords Project* in the West Texas/Southern New Mexico/Northern Chihuahua region. She continues to coordinate its free weekly workshops, occasional publications, and performance events in the El Paso area.

NeoPoiesis: *a new way of making*

1) in ancient Greece, poiesis referred to the process of making: creation - production - organization - formation - causation

2) a process that can be physical and spiritual, biological and intellectual, artistic and technological, material and teleological, efficient and formal

3) a means of modifying the environment and a method of organizing the self, the making of art and music and poetry, the fashioning of memory and history and philosophy, the construction of perception and expression and reality

4) an independent publisher with a steadfast goal to print and promote outstanding poets, writers and artists that reflect the creative drive and spirit of the new electronic landscape

NeoPoiesisPress.com